THIMK

5512-LOPE

THIMK

Vincent Lopez

5512-LOPE

Copyright © 2001 by Vincent Lopez.

Library of Congress Number: 2001117907
ISBN #: Hardcover 1-4010-2276-6
Softcover 1-4010-2275-8

All rights reserved. No part of this book may be reproduced or transmitted in any form or by any means, electronic or mechanical, including photocopying, recording, or by any information storage and retrieval system, without permission in writing from the copyright owner.

This book was printed in the United States of America.

To order additional copies of this book, contact:
Xlibris Corporation
1-888-795-4274
www.Xlibris.com
Orders@Xlibris.com

CONTENTS

5512-LOPE

PART II - LIF

5512-LOPE

*To Mom for putting up with me for all of these years. Love ya!

*To my best friends, McIver Willoughby Sr. (1930-1992) and Michael Lancaster (1980-1999) – I still feel you two with me everyday. Thanks for teaching me compassion and being there for me. We'll meet again for sure.

*To Shannon Harmon (1972-1997) the beautiful girl I first met way back in 1984 at Masterman whose hypnotic, soft eyes inspired me to start writing.

*To Dr. Cohen my fifth grade teacher at Masterman in 1982 who stayed on my case and was the first to say to me, "Vincent, THIMK!"

*To Sonia Sanchez – You're such a cool lady. Thanks for giving me an 'A' in your poetry class and telling me to never stop because you thought that I was good. You blew my mind when you said that!

*To all thimkers – I know that you're out there and I know that you're frustrated. It comes with the territory. Let's get together and thimk our way out of this madness. Together we can change this world.

5512-LOPE

And the thought of truth led me on.
And I walked after it and did not wander:
And all that have seen me were amazed:
And I was regarded by them as a strange person.

Odes of Solomon 17:5-6

INTRODUCTION

An older lady told me that when she read my words, she was taking a peek into my soul. A soul with worries and troubles of someone who had lived thousands of years. A soul with enough love for family, friends, enemies and strangers. A soul who spoke prophetically of times to come, interwoven with past and present events. This soul has years of experience but some who only identify with their outside don't understand my insides. They feel that my outside hasn't been around long enough. Sometimes this form doesn't comprehend what is within it. But those who know what I feel know what I'm saying and this peek into my soul may reveal a bit of your own to you.

5512-LOPE

PART I - *LUV*

YOU

For the beautiful, yet seemingly anonymous, young woman
Who by no effort or intent of your own
Caught my heart, held it, caressed it, and freed it
While staring at me smiling
And waving those smooth, delicate fingertips
Arousing all of my dormant passion, fire, and desire
Breathing in just the right amount of oxygen
As the rest of the nitrogen, argon, carbon dioxide, neon, and helium
Flowed through your dark follicles
Your eyes reflected the liquid brown African sun
Living within your soft shell
Causing my pulse to race . . . then, suddenly stop
This I must say to you, even though you may have no recollection or care
You charmed me, dazzled me, and gave me hope
All within those cherished five seconds of our destined meeting
I, a mere passer by
On your road of life
You, the only woman
Living within my skin.

STREETLIGHT

I lay down for a second
Then you called
I started thinking of
How you looked today
What you said
With your mouth
And your mind
I was thinking
Looking outside
Watching the rain fall
Onto the cement
Into little shining pools
Now I'm listening
To your voice
It's so sweet
I wish you were here now
With me
By the streetlight.

EVERY TIME

Women do it to you every time
They walk around with their walks
They look at you with those eyes
Delilah did it to Samson
Bathsheba did it to David
Queen of Sheba did it to Solomon
They wear that lipstick
They do it every time
They put on that sweet perfume
They wear that thought provoking attire
And wonder why you're staring?!
They curl their hair around their fingertips
Ever so slowly, gently
She's doing it again
They say things like, *"Hi"*
With those soft lips
Uttering that butter smooth voice
It gets me every time
Do you understand yet?
I get a little nervous sometimes
When I think about
Her
You try to conceal what you think
And how you feel
Because you don't want
To get got again
She did it anyway
Secretive. I might be
Lovable. Of course I am
Stubborn. Just a little
Romantic. In all 206 bones
Respectful. Don't leave home without it

Very intelligent also
But no matter what
She gets me every time
Been this way since about four years old
Had girlfriends in kindergarten
They even did it to me then
A little older now
A bit wiser, too
So I can control myself
You never know
When she might get you
When or where
But it's sure to happen sometime
She might creep up behind you at work
Write notes to you in class
She might call you at night
When you're lying in the bed
Alone
Thinking about her
She wants to be admired
She wants a lot of attention
But don't do it all the time
They'll take you for granted
And say, *"Let's just be friends"*
So when you're old and gray
Married to that sweet woman
Who is still as beautiful
As the day you first said to yourself
"Who! Is that?"
But she had that mean look on her face
And walked right by you that morning
The one who doesn't like you to have
Too many female friends
The one who you've kissed in your mind
One hundred forty-four thousand times

Her
Tell her that she got you every time
That you saw her
And spoke to her
Touched her
And she'll say, *"I knew it all the time!"*
How did she know?!?

LOVE YOUR WOMAN

Brothers love your girl
For when she's not there
Only you know
How many tears
Streamed down your face
In that cold bed
Brothers love your lady
For when she's not around
Your image in the mirror
Appears as half a man
Brothers love your woman
Truly she was made for you
Hold and kiss her tenderly
While thanking God always
Brothers love your woman
Love your woman
Love her.

BETWEEN FRIENDS

Quiet conversation
In my room
Sitting in the park
Taking pictures of her
Going to the movies
Talking on the phone
All night
Meeting each other's family
Kissing in the rain
In my mind
Helping her take off her shoes
Looking into each other's eyes
Just spending time together
As friends.

5512-LOPE

A CASUAL THOUGHT

Will I always love
And care for her
Will we always be
Spiritually attached
It feels that way
Sometimes
I miss the smile
Holding my hand
And the gentle laughter
Life is the most
Precious gift
And to have
Never ever
Loved someone
In your short lifetime
Would be sad
Some might question
Or wonder
If you ever really
Lived at all.

THE WOMAN OF . . .

I respect
The woman of chastity
Who cherishes her sacred womanhood
Instead of giving it
To unworthy scavengers
Who care nothing for her soul
I get chills from
The woman of determination
Who quietly walks my way
Without being seen or heard
With a lady's finesse
And a little girl's smile
In an attempt
To get to know my mind
I admire
The woman of motherhood
Single and young
Who's tired and broke
And just wants to get away
If only for a minute
Sacrificing herself for her children
So that they are taken care of
She demands and receives
My love and full support
I want
The woman of my dreams
I need
The woman of my reality
Who's fed up with "boy" friends
And playing childish games
She wants and needs a man
That sincerely wants and needs her

To grow, love, raise children, and be
Together
For worse or for better
Where are you woman?

UNDERGROUND EXPECTATIONS

The love I feel
Is too strong
For this pen and ink
To handle
My brown skinned woman
To give you one more second
On this dying planet
I'd shorten my own time
But now
You willingly give
Your days away
With your body and mind
In constant decay
The combination of syllables
Spewing from your tongue
Are the same
Tired and thoughtless
Brothers approach you
With hollow heads
In search of the womanhood
Hidden within your temple
And since these are your
Expectations also
Your palace is ravaged
Its' contents
That of every thing
On Earth
The Creator's perfect creation
Man's partner
Why is your mind

So far underground
Leaving your body
A helpless clone misguided
I see so much within you
I want so much for you
My reflection
My helpmate
Woman you send me
I hope I reach you soon.

HER

My life was never
As simple as grandma thought
"Find you a nice girl

To settle down with."
To me, women were bad luck
Like strange calls at twelve-

-After nine long months
"Buy me this, love me later."
All I ever heard

So player I was
Who could tell me about love
'Til she came along

She was Love to me
The personification
A Libra woman

Eyes shined pure brown fire
Hair and skin seeped mango juice
Voice chimed from gold chords

Had me, *ME!* panting
She called me nice, called me sweet
Never called me back

What was I to do
Sent messages by e-mail
I practically

Owned the flower shop
But still it wasn't enough
"Is this payback God?

Did I do her wrong?"
I contemplated my fate
Destined loneliness

'Til one month later
I just had to call that girl
"Need to talk to you

I've been thinking that . . .
I've never . . . I mean . . . I just . . .
I don't know how to . . ."

Ilyasha replied
"I was just about to call
I need your love, too."

IS IT . . .

Is it my smile
That gives you a tingle
Up and down all thirty-three
Sections of your delicate spine
Is it my mind
That you'd like to
Get better acquainted with
Or my hidden fifth pocket
Is it my love
That you crave
In the middle of the night
When you toss and turn
In need of healing
Is it my quiet strength
That comforts you
And makes you feel at ease
When the limpid fluid secretes
From the lachrymal gland
Is it my hands
That massage your back
After a long, hard day at work
Is it that my eyes
Aren't fixated on your behind
Each time you turn your head
Is it that I long
To hear your voice
To soothe, caress, and teach me
Is it that I walk up to you
Slowly and kiss you
Right there on your spot
Is it that our souls
Have been together

Since the Earth was void of life
Are you sure it's me you want
Or is it . . .

INCUBATE

My love for her grows
Like the chick in the brown shell
Longing for sunshine.

JUST TALK (FIRST ENCOUNTER)

Hey baby, what's your name
My name ain't baby
Well, I was just commenting
On how smooth your skin looks, Ms.
Ms. is what you may call me
Well Ms. Miss how are you today
I was fine until a few moments ago
I'm sorry I was a few seconds late
But I'm here now
Lord, please not today
Why Ms. Miss, what do you
Mean by that
I just want to get to know such
A fine specimen of The Creator
I don't have the time right now
Then I'll call you
I don't have a phone
You can call me
I don't think so
I'll just walk with you then
So that I may admire your
Exquisite beauty
Is that all right
It's a free world isn't is
Yeah, I guess it is
By the way my name is—
That's unimportant
Why is that
Because I don't want to know it
Okay then,

I love your hair Ms.
Really
I love your voice, too
Uh huh
Your skin is perfectly toned
Are you married
By any chance
Why do you ask
Because if you aren't
Then I'd like to ask for your hand
You must be out of your mind
You don't even know me
But it seems as if
I've known you for centuries
How's that
You just give off this comforting vibe
And I can't resist it
I bet you could if you started
Walking the other way
No I can't imagine life
Separated from you
Now that we've met again
What do you mean, again
I've never met you before
On the contrary
We met last night in my dream
You said you loved me
Before and after we kissed
Where did we kiss
First we were in my grandmother's backyard
Planting flowers
You stood up, walked over to me
And planted your lips on mine
What happened after that
Then I woke up to go to the bathroom

But when I fell asleep again
We were at the beach alone
Watching the sky while the sun went down
That's when you told me you loved me
That must have been a dream
Because I sure don't love you
How can you say that
After all we've been through
Excuse me
We have been through
One walk down the street
So that I could catch the bus
Which by the way is coming now
Goodbye
Wait don't leave me yet
I'll drive you home in my Mercedes
Where is it
Oh yeah, I forgot it's in the shop
But I'll get it out next week
Why do y'all always have to lie
I'd never lie to you sweetheart
When will I see you again
I don't know and I don't care
See you tomorrow then
Same time, same place
Men.

FROM AFAR

I admire her from afar
I see her on the corner
Getting into her car
Talking on the phone
At her desk
Typing on the computer
She seems so innocent
And at the same time unpredictable
She has smiled at me
On many Monday mornings
Eating a raisin bagel
Or drinking chamomile tea
But she doesn't know
That I long to hold her hand
Give her piggyback rides
And massage her feet
My mind wants to meet her
But my body isn't listening
Why are my limbs so shy
And afraid of rejection
I wish that I could speak to her
Using telepathy
But I haven't mastered it yet
So I must use
The old-fashioned approach
The *"Hello. How are you doing?"*
The *"I've seen you around."*
And the *"What's your name?"*
I hate these meaningless mind games
But I have to do something
To find out if she's the one
So I'll do it tomorrow

No today
I'm tired of being alone
And longing for her from afar.

THE GODDESS IN BLUE

A normal day
Really
I wasn't feeling too well
At five a little tired
A bit hungry
But alas I was going to meet
A goddess
With a sexy smile
And sweet, dangerous eyes
That could read the inspection sticker
On my soul
Left there by an angel
When I was first created
She let me in and walked away
All I could think was
She's different
She has her own style
And she's fine
I could feel her essence
Coaxing me to follow
The soft steps made by pink cotton
We spoke for a minute
And soon it was time to go
Too soon I thought
The chit chat in the dark
By the door
Before I left
Made me fully realize
She truly is a goddess
With her braids pulled back
Just the way I like
Her stature perfect

Her bone structure
Reminiscent of Nefertiti
Maybe Cleopatra
Her skin glowed in the dim light
While I stared at her silently
And of course those divine portals
Directly below her sleek eyebrows
I was trying to take it all in
So of course I couldn't speak much
This woman with quiet strength
And a shell hardened by society
I feel is the sweetest little girl inside
Who just needs to be free
I can't wait until
My next encounter with this
Goddess in blue.

WHAT A COOL BREEZE DID

My love for her will cease
When the sea smooths out
Its last wrinkle
And as the seagull skims the skin
Of a river's surface
For a morsel which fell
From the sky
So I dip my mind's pen
Into the inkblood of my heart
With sincere intent
Followed by a sigh.

WHY?

When I'm at work
Why do I want her?
When I'm in the bed
Why can't I sleep?
When I'm in the shower
Why do I feel lonely?
When I call
Why isn't she there?
When I write
Why does she control the pen?
When I'm driving
Why do I see her in the car next to me?
When I'm holding her
Why don't I want to let go?
When I kiss her
Why does it feel like I'm in another universe?
Forgive me. I can't seem to forget her
Why?

KISS SHE BLUE

Blue^3: Part 1

The twinkle in her eye
I first saw in '84
The tender sparkle in her eye
I first saw in '84
Young and innocent then
Before destiny knocked at the door

Used to follow her around
And watch from over there
Would sneak all around
To catch a glimpse from right there
She never knew that her beauty
Would on my cheek leave a tear

At twelve years old she possessed
Charm, grace, and the like
Just twelve years old and she harnessed
Charisma, sweetness, and the like
And when the lunch bell rang
To sit near her, us boys would fight

Made up my mind to tell her
How much I adored her so
I just had to tell her
That I truly loved her so
With paper, a number 2 pencil
My heart let fly its arrow

I didn't know if she received it
Asked my friend, *"Who'd you give it to?"*
Wasn't sure if she had read it
Asked Sekou, *"Who'd you give it to?!?"*
Hung my head low and began to cry
Dreamed of a kiss she blue

The twinkle in her eye
I first saw in '84
The tender sparkle in her eye
I first saw in '84
Young and innocent then
Before destiny knocked...

BLUE FUNK

Blue³: Part 2

Damn baby
Said DAMN woman
Said DAMN GIRL
9TEEN
What happened to
You…You…You…
TurnedmehimthemANDEVENHEROUT!!!
The memories too much to bear
Wet Kisses, Skin-tight hugs, Raspberry body-oil rubs
Vanilla cream whipped with strawberries, grapes, Yams and Pickles!?!
Two three four of us
Every four to six hours
Like Tylenol, Advil, DayNyquil
You didn't start that way
That sweet smile turned sour
You know not…
Wait
You do know what you do when you do how you do
But do you know WHY YOU DO
I feel I need I feel
I WANT NEED YOU
But you ain't ready
You…
Found another
AAHHHHH!!!
He's got you now girl
He'd got you
Be careful lady
Not TOOOO FAST

He's tricky baby
Slooooowww down
But then you thought you needed more
And more
And MORE
Much more than you wanted he gave…

BLACK AND BLUE

Blue^3: Part 3

The last time I cried
Was when I saw her face
The very last time I cried
Was when I saw her face
And lips touching another man
On the steps of her place

I remember when
She would hold me that tight
Oh, I remember when
She would hold me that tight
Hypnotized by her brown eyes
I never put up a fight

He didn't seem to know either
What she could do to him
Said he didn't seem to know either
What she could do to him
In the grip of that lioness
Things looked mighty grim

That sly woman met her match
A man with a wicked mind
That cunning woman met a horrible match
A man with a wicked mind
Entranced her with his stare
And made evil seem kind

The glow has left her face
And her limbs are stiff and cold
The soft glow has left her face
And her limbs are stiff and cold
The lion devoured the lioness
'Cause an untruthful story she told

The last time I cried
Was when I saw her face
The very last time I cried
Was when I saw her face
And lips beaten still and silent
I swear it was a disgrace.

06/18/98

Sometimes
I meet a woman
With deep emotional
Scars
And a mind beaten
To such a weary submission
That I can see
Bandages on her soul.

UNTIL FURTHER NOTICE

To my left
Last night
Yes
The day before this one
While absorbing universal thoughts
At a poetry reading
In October Gallery
I saw Her again
About seven wooden folding chairs over
Exchanging passionate peeks
The Most High's aura surrounded Her
And the vibe was so strong
I felt it earlier that day
Toiling away at work

She sat alone peaceably
As I felt myself
Departing slowly
Staring at Her
In five second intervals
Feeding my lonely desire
But I just couldn't seem to . . .
. . . Get around those people
"What about, 'Excuse me'"
. . . Get my free poster
"Like you really wanted it"
. . . Get up the nerve
"That's what I thought"
This shyness makes my body
Freeze and focus
On anything and everything
Except that special sister

I glanced Her way
Before my friend and I
Stepped out
Into the breezy night air
I told Her
That I loved Her
That I missed Her
That she was as beautiful as forever
And that I'd speak up soon
All of that from
Thirty feet
And thirty people away
Without these lips parting once

My flesh is the assailant
And my soul is too often
An innocent victim
So until further notice
My heart is closed
For repairs.

THE BEHOLDER

Thoughts only take
A few seconds to form
But they are beyond
The realm of time
The sight of a maiden
With skin the complexion
Of the tents of Kedar
And the voice
Of a cool spring wind
Invades the very cytoplasm
Of my cells
Giving me enough strength
To pull up Lemuria
From the depths of the sea
Giving me the desire
To send you sweet messages
Throughout the day
By carrier pigeon
Carefully inscribing each word
On an evaporating
Particle of moisture
I saw you yesterday
No take that back
I feel you everyday
With the natural
Switch and sway of your hips
Keeping me in a trancelike state
When I hear your shoes
Tap, tap, tap
Along the sidewalk
Across the street
Down the hall

All I can do is gulp
Because my breath has left me
Your distinct scent
Draws me toward you
Enlivening my senses
Like animal pheromones
Hypnotize the beasts of the field
Mine eyes have yet
To witness the glory
Of the coming of The Lord
But a creation such as you
Humbly hearkens me
To be patient
While beholding
Your exquisite majesty.
Selah

WOUNDED IN THE HOUSE OF A FRIEND

Walking up the front steps
As usual politeness went first
Me second
And the mysterious force guarding my back last
The doorbell was pressed
And obviously so was I
Since hearing those words
Most brothers hate to hear
"We have to talk."
Ever apparent confidence
Dwindled to the nervous
Questioning of every past step
Sat down quietly
Hands folded on my lap
Never did that before
She walked quietly down the stairs
With the scent of Mango incense
Floating closely behind
Dressed in Grey Gap sweatpants and shirt
Hair in a ponytail
Red perfume by Giorgio
Brown sandals exposing
Toenails painted a natural tone
Almost felt a tear glide down my right cheek
I thought, *"Damn, she looks so good!"*
Her voice sounded as sweet
As the strawberry lip gloss
Glistening in the dim light
Ears impatient and twitching to hear
Those seven words

My mind wasn't prepared to listen to
"I think we should just be friends."
Confusion and hurt graffitied on my face
Heart stopped beating
Murder was the case
I pretended not to care
No, *"What, when, why, or where?"*
Picked it up off the floor
Me first went out the door.

FIND ME

If I walk this Earth
Once more
Just once
Without seeing you
Feeling you
I will burst
Into 1,532,647,724 dark brown ants
Scattering to find a new home
A new queen
A new love
I'm taking my last few breaths
Now
So find me before I fall
Into the ground
And fly back to the Creator.

WELL…

I like women
That stimulate my mind
More than my eyes
You know your sight
Gets worse with age.

WONDERING WHO

I'm always
Thinking of you
You're always
Thinking of me
Wondering who
Each other is
Wondering where
Each other is
Wondering when
We'll finally meet
Many days and nights
Have been spent
Wondering
You know who you are
I know who I am
But why
Haven't we met yet
Or maybe we've
Seen each other
Already
And we did not
Realize it was us
It tears me up inside
Knowing you're out there
And I know
You feel the same
I miss you
I want to hold you
But I'm not even sure
Who you are
I live for the
Love of you

And you only
I lay alone
In my bed
At night
Staring into the blackness
Watching
Those weird stars
Trying to form
Your picture
In my mind
I know you do the same
You are beautiful
Intelligent and sweet
I know that much
So why can't we
Be together now
Instead of
Wondering
What
Where
When
Why
Who?

ORDINARY PAIN

Our paths crossed one day
Under a magnificent skyline
That only The Most High
Could have created
This male water and dust
Came across a woman
Not an ordinary woman
A sweet, delicate woman
That needs to be held and caressed
Without speaking a word
I'll do whatever it takes
To ease her tender spirit
She has two of the most
Spectacular portals to the soul
As keen and sharp as a razor
They shine, glow, and speak
Words, thoughts, and emotions
Barely explainable
But wholeheartedly felt
Her distinctive style and approach
Are those of a cheetah
Calm, smooth, and sure
Of what's she's looking for
So as I write this
Expressing what I feel
All of my pain
The pain I've felt
Since being separated
From the umbilical cord
Has rescinded
And poured out of my
Chest and skull

She has made me whole again
Two have become one
And what The Creator
Binds together
Shall never come undone.

CONTINENTAL DIVIDE

doyouknow
howlongisearched
forasistertolove
doyoureallyknow
thosethatdidnotgivemetimeofday
andawordinedgewise
say
ididntsearchlongenough
hardenough
farenough
wideenough
ihearthemSCREAMATME!!!
butwhatamitodo
whenmysearchisunsuccessful
whenimtiredofwaitinginvain
invain
invain
whenanotherwoman
bornonanothercontinent
driftstome
iafricakidnapped
sheasiavoluntary
whatamitodo
whenmylonelybleedingheart
latchesontoonewhoresemblesnotasister
icantlikecantloveher?
icanttalktoandholdher?
momma
whatamitodo
whenmylovereachesout
tosomeoneoppositeofme
andoppositeofyou???

VISIONS

Were we in love
At least I was
And last night
When you came to me
In a vision
We held each other
So
I know we miss
One another
We talked
And hugged
And held hands
And kissed
And talked some more
And upon awakening
I even cried
'Cause I know that
We were meant
But not right now
Not in this lifetime
You returned too soon
I used to think
But who am I
To question
Your return
To the astral plane
So since you've been gone
I've seen you only
In these visions
Of pure love energy
When these alpha/beta waves
Blip uncontrollably

5512-LOPE

When my limbs shake
And heart beats faster
And my ectoplasm leaves
To join you there
I know you know
I miss you
I really do miss you
'Til I close my eyes again
And you come to me
In a vision.

SHANNON HARMON
March 4, 1972-September 7, 1997

WHEN LOVE SILENTLY SITS AND WATCHES

I've been looking
For her
Pondering her whereabouts
Calling her name
But hearing no sound
'Cause love's been silent

I feel her presence
Amongst the city's shadows
And like a homing device
I try to close in
On her position
But soon she disappears
Always a second ahead of me

What is it that I should do
Do I hold you woman
In too high a regard
Have I discovered things
In your heart
You didn't know were there

I'd have no power
Were it not for your shining eyes
Burning deep into my soul
I'd feel no hope
Were it not for your fingertips
Caressing my flesh while I sleep

When your electromagnetic energy

Seeps from the atmosphere
Into me
I feel ripples beneath my skin
Causing my heart
To pump blood cells
In the shape of your name

As you stride the planet
Like the lioness on the prowl
My body freezes
Like Han Solo
In the carbonite
Your voice is like
An orchestra of raindrops
Slowly, steadily soothing my tension

I know you're out there
On this same globe
Woman
Constantly eluding me
If I continue to live
This sad life
Full of unused love
My tombstone will read
"He loved her but she never knew
Because love silently sat
And watched him suffer."

WOM*B*AN

Wom*b*an
Why you
Criss cross quietly
By me, by me
Make me
Make me
Wanna reach out
To your five extremities
Speak out
To your inner psychic
Being
That naturally
Shining crown of
Real Earth grown hair
That vibrant skin
Of melanin
That *"makes me wanna*
Do thy bidding" smile
Those eyes so bright
So gentle
So caring
So you
Wom*b*an…
Why you
Criss cross quietly
By me,
by me?

STOLEN MOMENTS

I will never forget them
I cherish every moment
In my mind
I'd be without purpose
Were it not for them
At their mere mention
I feel like a helpless
Weak child
No logic or intellect
Can shield you from the aura
Of a true Wisdom
Queasy stomach and clouded mind
Can't even think clearly
I simply adore them
Want them
Need them
When your body feels as if it
Will break into pieces
And drift away
Like the islands and continents
It can only be one thing
Pure and simple
Your better half
The awesome power
Of
Woman.

WHERE HAVE ALL OF THE GOOD GIRLS GONE?

It's been some time now
Since I've seen her
The heart fluttering
Doe-eyed girl
Her voice was…
Was…
Gentle
As a mother robin
Awakening her young
I miss
Us walking together
Our fingers engulfed
In Braille conversation
Our eyes inhaling
Each other's image
I miss
Us lying together
Fully clothed
But feeling so close
Sharing long hidden secrets
Making space
In a cluttered closet
As old bones turned to ash
I miss
Us hugging
Two warm bodies
Interlocking
Like long lost puzzle pieces
She was one of the last
Good girls

In search of…
In need of…
Me, I hoped
Where have you gone sweet woman
Where have all of you good girls
Gone?

☺☺☺☺☺☺☺SMILE☺☺☺☺☺☺☺

You
Smiled at me
Woman
And I smiled back
Since then…
Girl
I just ain't been the same

Your face
Your smile
Imprinted on my mind
Like a tattoo
Like a distant jet
Flying in circles
Waaaay up high
Making clouds in the sky
You're there

In the four, three, two seconds
It took for me to walk by
When your lips said, *"Hi"*
When your hair spoke
Swahili, Italian, Japanese, Hieroglyphics
Each strand containing
It's own cryptic definition
Of the word love

You
Just calming standing there
Smiling
And I sloooowly melted
Like the wild cherry and

Blueberry Rita's water ice
On July 15
But you didn't see
That
And you didn't know
That
I wanted to say
"Goddess
Brown-skinned lady
Mother of my small u-n-I-verse
Your smile
Your sweet, sweet smile
Made me feel…
Made me feeeeeeel
Made me think
Made me want
The essence
The being
The very heart of
You."

10% DIS

For the woman who glided by
With the paralyzing soft scent
Who lynched my vocal chords
Allowing only silent phrases to escape their home
The woman who telekinetically moved
My right index and forefinger to my left wrist
Checking for blue, purple, red, *ANY* blood pressure
The woman whose sienna brown thick, curly locks
Radiated all of the unknown secrets of the universe
And the exact milli-second of my conception
The woman who made the nervous twitch
In the inner thigh above my knee return
The woman whose caramel coated skin
Alluded to the same taste in her lips
This woman said nothing and everything in three clicks
As she passed by
Her cute nose turned upward and away
Her eyes fixed on some pigeon decorating a car
In her mind I was but a gnat
And she the tigress
Showing me in all her glory
That she truly was but an ass

No dreds
No white gems
Or big muscles
Just me
My specs
Light brown eyes
Calm demeanor
And love for thee.

IF ONLY YOU KNEW

This is my way
Of communicating
My thoughts
And feelings
I thought you knew
You want me to talk
But understand something
Woman
You give me butterflies
Right here *(put right hand on heart)*
I smile and laugh just as much
As you
But I'm still a little shy
I thought you knew
There are so many things
That I want you to know
So many questions
I'd like to answer
But I must be patient
Because I want . . .
If only you knew.

5512-LOPE

COINCIDENCE?

...And in that instant
That swift moment
As my legs
And feet moved forward
With momentum
Your eyes orbited
Thirty degrees west
Five degrees north
And met mine
The conversation they shared
Across photon beams
At 5:01:27 Earth time
Six months on the mental plane
Too short
At parting
As my legs
And feet moved forward
With momentum
I felt
And beheld
The visage
Of a mocha brown
Sweet maiden
Your configuration
On astrological charts
The placement
Of celestial bodies
Biblical prophecy
And as my legs
And feet moved forward
With momentum
And gravity

Held me firm
To the sidewalk
My memory rewound
Back to that millisecond
The sight of orbiting eyes
And what a coincidence
That at that time
And space
In the Milky Way galaxy
I saw
The lovely you.

EVERY TIME (THEY DO IT)

The "All By My Lonesome" Rewrite Remix

Women
Still do it every time
To keep you on edge
Is my guess
Crossing the black tar
Between corners
She locked eyes with me
Like we had each other on radar
But she kept on stepping
Expecting me to what
Follow?
I almost did
She sure looked good
With kissable lips and thick thighs
They do it
Coasting down Broad Street
Near Temple
I saw her standing on the yellow
Pausing to get a glimpse
Of a smooth chocolate sister
She looked at me with that
"Why don't you get out
Of the car and kiss me fool?"
Facial expression
Almost making me crash
Into students, cars, and poles
They do it to you
At the market
I saw her examining fruit
Not too far from me

She started squeezing oranges
And lemons
Tasting grapes
Delicately placing them
Into her mouth slooooowly
Peering at me
Twinkling her eyes
I knew I shouldn't have
Gotten a carryall basket
It fell right on my foot
They know how to do it
Tossing and turning
Under the covers
I smell her perfume
Shampoo and body oil
In my dreams
Telling me to call
Come over
So we can talk?
Still doing it to me
What's a man to do
When he can't find that woman
But thinks he sees her everyday
They all are one
But they all can't be
"The One"
Can they?
One thing's for sure though
They do it to me
Every time.

TEENAGE LOVE

November 24, 1990
Mood: Lonely
Time: 12:40AM

Vincent,

If I write this letter over again, I think I'll scream! So I promised myself this is the last time.

Before when you left for college, I really didn't have anything to say. It was like I turned around and you were gone. No last minute goodbye or anything. I didn't realize how much I missed you until Wednesday. You look much better to me anyway with your hair cut like it is now, than in a box. Even my mom thinks so.

You can't tell me that none of those girls up there don't try to talk to you. Because I know I would. But then again you are kinda porky there. You know, for a person that always complains about nasty food. It must not be too nasty!

I think you have Johnny Gill's tape but if not borrow it and listen to the fourth song on side B. Well, I really didn't have much to say because the song and the poem on the next page sums just about all have to say up. So enjoy and I miss you!

Hugs & Kisses
Nikki

Afraid

When I met you,
I was afraid to look at you
When I looked at you,
I was afraid to kiss you

When I kissed you,
I was afraid to love you
Now that I love you,
I'm afraid of losing you.

JUST TALK (NOT HIM AGAIN)

Hey baby
I mean hello Ms.
Remember me
I'm Russell from yesterday
How are you on this fine day
I know I'm feeling better now
Since you've graced me with your presence
Oh, it's you again
Don't you work somewhere
Yes, I do work but only for you
Well why haven't I seen the money yet
Because I'm investing it to buy our home
Our home? I don't think we'll be living together
You women sure are moody
Changing your minds all the time
Yesterday you loved me
And today you don't know me
I'm hurt now
That's not my fault
You need to find a woman
Who really wants you
You are that woman
The woman I want to be mine
You fine, sexy lady
With your hair pulled back
And your fingernails painted
I could just
Wait a minute now, Mr. Russell
Let's get this straight right now
Y-O-U are not my kind of man

You may be cute
And dressed nicely
But I'm not attracted to you
So you think I'm cute, huh
Most women do
I get my looks from my mother
And this curly hair
From my Cherokee grandfather
I knew you loved me, Ms. Miss
Can you hear at all
Am I talking to a wall
Yes, I heard your voice
But your heart keeps saying
"Russell, Russell, Russell
He's the one for me."
You just don't want to tell me yet
But that's all right
I like shy women
Russell, I have to go now
Have a nice day
You do the same my love
See you tomorrow.

YOU AGAIN

For the captivating
Yet seemingly mysterious YOUng woman
Who by no kinetic intent of YOUr own
Captured my heart
While standing innocently there
Emitting enlivening sweet scents of enchantment
Lifting slowly from perfect honey brown pores
Arousing all of my dormant passion
Forgetting my pain, my meager existence
YOU standing there
The she panther
YOUr eyes reflecting the psychic kisses
I blew secretly to YOUr lips
As I walked casually by
Coming and going
My pulse racing . . . then suddenly . . .
This I must say to YOU, even though YOU may have no recollection or care
YOU moved me, moved me!
This man normally a stone
I become a raindrop in YOUr presence
Hoping to fall into YOUr soft hand
The five seconds we've shared on planet Terra
Have truly meant something
As these words
From my heart, brain and fingertips
Mean everything
I, a mere passer by
On YOUr road of life
YOU, the only woman
Living within my skin.

PART II - *LIF*

THE FORCE OF WATER

The waves
Oh, the churning waves
Of that great blue ocean
Rocking this monstrous wooden beast
Brown like me
I've just been whipped
But I feel pain
No more
I feel not the shackles
On my wrists
Around my neck and ankles
I think not of my brother
Who jumped recently
See, he felt not the pain
But the warmth
Of the big fish that swallowed him
Now I lie here
Next to my new family
Cramped together
Feces and urine
Creating a thick paste
I smell it not
Right next to me
My brother has passed out
His wound so deep
I can see the chalk white
Of his shoulder blade
Rubbing against the hard plank
But still I see it not
As I meditate in this hell
I see only
The beauty of my long lost home

I hear only
My mother's soothing voice
I taste only
The sweet yams of the Earth
I smell only
The fragrant oil of my wife's hair
I feel only
The churning waves
Of that great blue ocean
Rocking this monstrous wooden beast
Brown like me.

ACROSS THE STREET, AROUND THE CORNER

I live across the street
From his mother
He lives around the corner
From my mine
I kinda thought that was strange
We said our *"What's up?"*
When we crossed
He saw me come home from work
And knew I wasn't about B.S.
He respected that
I knew what he was about, too
Illusory tough guy
Nickels and dimes
Of whatever your pleasure
Was he means
Of consolidating currency
Can't knock the hustle

Across the street
I watched women
Visiting at all hours
I'd stand outside
On the porch
Listening to arguments and screams
Saw girls running out crying
With him cursing behind
He'd watch girls
Visit my abode, too
No strange noises to be heard
Just hearty laughs
And movies in stereo

Around the corner
I'd sit on my mother's step
Conversing with some shortie
He'd cruise by
Or walk around
We'd nod heads
And he'd go up the street
To argue with the other
Young brothers in competition
Burners pulled
But they ain't want none
And neither did he
Too much damn television
Was my conclusion

Across the street
I'd see him pull up
In car, in van, in jeep
With the same phenomenally beautiful
And abused female
He had many wheels
I only had four
His mom would come out
Smokin' a cigarette
Shakin' her head
She never worked
My guess
The dope impaired her
And he was the supplier

Around the corner
Young brothers were itchin'
Hungry, angry
The week before

They watched as the cement
And cinder blocks
Shut the eyes of their hell hole
Suspecting him
The letters spelling
R.E.V.E.N.G.E.
Swam in their blood
Like alphabet soup

Across the street
I haven't seen him
In two weeks
Heard he was in an accident
Broken leg
Three places
He still drove around
Cast and all in that big van
Brothers love to profile

Around the corner
As he was driving home
Pedigree not stray
Bullets
Pierced, shredded
The van's cheap material
And his strong melanated skin
Striking him high and low
He parked in front of his home
Took that last breath too soon
And returned alone
To fill out his time card
Mission unaccomplished

Across the street
I saw his mother
Returning from the funeral
Didn't look too upset
Maybe she was hiding it
The pain, grief
Second and third guesses
Of what was done wrong
She lost a son
Who is remembered
For unnoble deeds
Tough guys live in two places
Some in metal and stone cages
And him
Well he lives with the others
In a huge garden
Called a cemetery
Under the grass and soil
I live across the street
From his mother
He *lived* around the corner
From mine.

IN MY WORLD

If we all are one
Within this cosmos
And on this planet
Why does everyone
Appear to be a fraction

Two-fifths shot seven-eights
Three-fourths robbed nine-tenths
One-half was cheating on one-fourth
And now he has two more mouths to feed
Four-fifths and six-sevenths
They're fraternal twins

No particular
Form, fashion, method
To this madness
Those less financially endowed
Are incarcerated
For being just that
Those of the world
Are sentenced to serve
Impoverished communities
Something they should have done
From the beginning

The universal laws
We pretend not to know of
Common sense
We pretend not to have
It being outlawed long ago
We follow other
Traditions

Rituals
Directions
And footsteps blindly
Into the cold earth

I see tears in defense
Of religious emotional ties
But they're not strong enough
To replace thought waves and truth

My people have persevered
Throughout centuries of turmoil
And their blood and sweat
Is like compounded interest
Growing within our skin
So the world really is ours
For the taking

Many say they're tired
At youthful ages these days
Some comment
"These children are lazy"
But they've inherited
Unused sleep
Which lied within southern fields
Waiting to return home

I remember hearing
"We shall overcome"
But did anyone
Internalize the thought
Overcome racism
Poverty
Homelessness
What?

We must overcome
OURSELVES
Or they will be ordering
Formaldehyde for you, too

Many beautiful children
Have ugly thoughts
And twisted minds
Dying before realizing
What life is
In my world.

UNINTENTIONAL

Shaded gray wings
Carried a chubby pigeon
To the littered black tar
A nano second later-
Heard a quick snap, crack, or pop
A trail of feathers
In my rear view
A little soul
Flew through the sky
When my sixty dollar Goodyear
Tipped its hat
"Hello, Goodbye."

M.E.A.T.
(MAN EATS ANY THING)

Cows mostly eat grass
But man's infinite wisdom
Says to eat the cows

"Eat cows, die faster"
Every doctor knows this
But won't tell us that

People get sicker
So doctors prescribe more drugs
Body gets weaker

Antibiotics
Make immune system break down
Make doctor richer

Buy Pepto Bismol
For heartburn and stomach pains
Body says, *"Please stop!"*

But you still eat cows
Soon the doctor's greed kills him
And the cow kills you

Reincarnation
Now the cow has become you
And you become cow

Doctor becomes grass

Digested in cow's stomach
Grass becomes shit

Fertilizes soil
Finally . . . his debt repaid?
Comes back as a cow!!!

THE SHELL GAME

Chained to the rock
Like Prometheus
While a ravenous world
Pecks at my
Withering sanity
I faintly hear a soft whisper
In the concentrated melanin
Of my eardrums
Gird up thy loins
Young man
Time is of the essence
I carefully place
The breastplate of righteousness
Across my sternum
And the helmet of salvation
Onto my cranium
It is time now
To play the shell game
I must protect myself
For the stakes of this game
Are loss of coherent thought
Respect torn from the core
Of an etheric fist-sized organ
And finally physical disintegration
You see the shells
Of this game aren't calcareous
The shells of this game
Aren't moved swiftly about
Under the palm of a hand
You see the shells of this game
Every day
Walking to and fro

In a dream like state
Some who inhabit shells
Think
Not too much or too deep
But nonetheless
Think
That because they inhabit
A particular combination
Of atoms
That form cells
That form tissues
That form organs
That form shells
Like the one you're in now
The one you think is you
They think that
They deserve special attention
Recognition, praise, favors
And what have you
But it's what's inside
That counts
And reads and writes
And cries and fights
Not the machine you control
But the soul.

THE THINGS THAT HAPPEN TO ME

On October 23, 1996
I had to take my car to the dealer
To get an overpriced radiator hose
Replaced in the engine
So I had to sit in the waiting room
For about three hours
Anticipating this
I brought my bookbag that contained
Some pad and paper to write down
Anything inspiring
A book to read
Tapes from my car since the mechanics
Like to steal
And most importantly
My crochet needle and yarn
Because I was making a blanket for someone
And I wanted to finish that ball of yarn
So I was sitting there
With three older Caucasian women
Two were watching television
And one was reading a book
And an African-American man in his mid to late 60's
They were watching Jenny Jones
And I was reading the newspaper
While the lady next to me kept glancing
My way with nervous jitters
I had on a gray Gap sweatsuit
A blue Gap hat
And brown Timberlands
And I hadn't shaved in awhile

So I guess I intimidated her
I felt like telling her
"If I wanted to take your pocketbook
Or your life I would have done it by now!
I'm here having my car serviced just like you!"
Anyway I looked up for a second
At the television
And there was an African-American male
On the screen
Making other African-American males look bad
Whatever he was saying
Made the ladies keep looking my way
While the one next to me kept saying
"Can you believe these people?"
So I said to myself
"Let me start crocheting this blanket
To dispel some of their ignorant stereotypes."
I pulled it out of my bag
And started crocheting like I was a grandmother
Very, very fast
Looking out of the corner of my eyes
I saw the older man to my left staring
At me in amazement
Then the scared woman to my right
Kept turning her head from the television back
To me with an astounded look on her face
As if she were watching a tennis match
After about five minutes
I was laughing so hard
On the inside that I couldn't
Control my face so I forced myself to smile
The lady on my right said to me
"You do that very well. I'm always
Bumbling around when I do it."
After saying this and seeing me smile

She finally relaxed
But kept looking at me as if it were a dream
I wanted to tell her to not make
Pre-judgments or comparisons of people
Based on their appearance
And what she saw on television
But I decided not to
Since I felt that she had already learned
A valuable lesson that day.

UNTITLED

Creator
Creator, would you please tell me this
Why is this world a hell
And not eternal bliss

My child
My child, before I tell you that
Is this brown Earth an orb
Or is your mother flat

Creator
Creator, how thus can I say
If the shape of your creation
Was made in which way

I've only stood on it
For twenty five years
She has fed me and clothed me
And absorbed all my tears

My child
My child, you are right to say
You don't know what the Earth
Looks like today

But some mosquitoes bring fever
To those that they sting
Even though they may pretend
To not know a thing

So my child
My child, what you ask you know well
How my children have turned heaven
Into their very own hell.

SEE AISLE SIT E

The breeze
Cool, calming
The waves
Swift, powerful
The ocean
Life itself
The way we were brought
My mind
Finally a piece of peace
I had to come
To the water
The water called me back
To this unknown
Little town
Mended my broken spirit
That force of water
Those birds fly so higgghhhhh…
Why can't we be
Like the water
The water that made us all.

ONE DAY

one day i'll
disappear
'cause this pain
is suffocating
debilitating
one day i'll
walk away
unnoticed
barely missed
'cause
these beings
can't be free
looking for this
and that
when they
are in front of themselves
one day i'll
transcend
all raindrops
cell structures
wind
sunshine
and be me
for real
free.

THEY LIVE

They live
Like vicious ants
Searching for a morsel
These humans we call African
And Black

Their love,
To me, is hate
See, they love to hate me
Anybody doing for self
Respect

This girl
I met for an
Example said to me
"I like you but you ain't my type."
Say what?!

Her type
Was the type that
Caressed skin with knuckles
Returned love with disappointment
And grief

I said
Right back at her
"You ain't my type either
But I care for you just the same,
Woman."

One guy
I grew up with

Told me behind my back
*"He's a sell out motherf@#*er
Working*

*All day
With white people."*
That brother looked like me
But potential held him hostage
Weekdays

Weekends
And soon after
Just a month later when
I visited him behind bars
He cried

They live
Like Evil's king
Of their minds, of their souls
These humans we call African
I love.

SUNDAY MORNING

I saw
His last smile
He saw
Not the gun
Or bullet.

BEST FRIENDS

(For McIver Willoughby Sr.—7/15/30—8/04/92)

As early as I can remember
I heard the phrases
"Hey, buddy!" or *"Hey, old man!"*
"What cha' know good?"
A soul spiritually attached to mine
By The Eternal
So we are forever
Best friends

He worked hard to support two families
And produced my mother
Who was "Daddy's Little Girl"
The positive male role model
Whom I called "grandpop"
Was in actuality one with myself

When the time came for his mission to end
I saw the peace and tranquility in his eyes
Now he no longer lives on the Earth
But like the rest of my true family
He lives within my heart

Graveyards hold no souls
Just wooden coffins full of dust
So I don't talk to tombstones
I talk to The All
No tears, No fears
One Creator, One Love.

THE PEN

So small and so light
Yet it has sent many
A human being
To gas chambers
Electric chairs
Lethal injections
And even to war
More people have died
As a result of ink
Than all of the earthquakes
Floods, tornadoes, and hurricanes
Ever
Some countries entire
Economic systems
Have been undermined
Due to certain individuals
Wielding this tiny sword
And conjuring evil thoughts
Pens have amassed more wealth
From looting vaults
Than all of the firearms ever created
Ironically you get less time
In prison
When you take more money with a pen
This writing utensil
Has been used to sign
Marriage licenses and divorce papers
For the same people
Birth and death certificates
Arrest and search warrants
And million dollar sports contracts
Yet and still

It stays quiet and humble
And always patient
I guess when you
Hold such concentrated power
Those who need assistance
Will come to you.

E-MAIL

The computer has become
Our faceless
Mediator and voyeur
Watching us reading
Each other's words
Watching us type
Our most intimate thoughts
Circuitry its organs
Electricity its blood
It loves not
But kills
Quietly emitting radiation
Why do we give
A stranger such power?

OFFER NO RESISTANCE

Why do we find
Such comfort in ignorance
And a harsh dislike
For our own selves

The pain we feel
Is only energy
Waiting to be transformed
Into the happiness
We thought we wanted

If we look inside
Our questions will be answered
We'll see our dreams in hibernation
Our hate will fear our newfound strength

But our own adversity
Our greatest stumbling block
Is us

We offer no resistance
Against ourselves
So we continue
This half-hearted struggle
And wonder why
Nothing has been changed
By one of, some of, any of
Us
Why not you

Now when I look
Into the children's eyes
I see heavy hearts
Swelled with liquid sorrow
Noble, original blood
With no knowledge of its origin

So it's all clear now
Our fight begins right here
Right now
Wherever you are
Stop
Look
Listen
And search
Deep within.

HAPPEE

All I really want
Is to be *happee*
All I really want
Is to just be free
Happee
Like the ant
Who found
A young girl's
Lost, wet lollipop
Happee
Like my momma
Leaving work early
On Friday
Happee
Like a pigeon
Pecking moldy, green
Wheat bread crumbs
Real *happee*
Sincere *happee*
Unconditional
No strings attached
Happee
For the moment
The breath
Each one
Coming and going
As it will
Without my thought interference
Why we make *happee*
So difficult
So stressful
To obtain

Maintain
Too much thinking
Ignorance is bliss
But ignorance ain't *happee*
Just blind
So where is *happee*
Who keeps *happee*
To theyself
Man, I was lookin'
For *happee*
All over the place
Thought *happee*
Was trapped
In glass bottles
In Philly blunts
In spewing cuss words
In wet cunts
Thought *happee*
Was like a genie
And I was gonna
Set *happee* free
Until one day
I woke up
And found *happee*
Was in me.

THE AWAKENING

I slowly ease my way up
Ascending quietly
From the dirty mortal frame
Free again
For a little while each night
As long as that prison sleeps

Oh how I despise being holed in
Like a Jinn in the lamp
But I appreciate the free time
I am given to explore
And meet others like me
Which that ignorant shell
Refers to as a dream

It's dark now
As I arise like a Phoenix
I am made of pure fire
Not Earth
So I need no rest
What is that I see
Watching the darkness silently
The glass coated with amalgam
Which watches and reflects
The undiffused dim light
Forming virtual images of
Every thing in this messy room
Except me

I've seen so many flesh creatures
During my travels on this plane
Staring blankly into

These convex and concave
Oval, round, and square
Pocket-size
Glued to ceilings and walls
Watching themselves
With disfigured facial expressions
Speaking and performing unimaginable acts
All is vanity here

They would rather gaze upon
An aging, decaying form
With bloodshot eyes
Painted with colored chemicals
And sprayed with unnatural scents
Than to look within
To find the true self
The misuse of these objects
Have caused many to resort
To plastic, silicon, and regurgitating
Even razor blade tracks
Across wrists and jugulars

I've seen many of my lost family
Being dragged down into that fiery pit
The Hell that they created
Weeping and screeching at the horror
About to befall them
Because of deeds done in the
Presence of the heated sand

The ways are wicked here
And the end will soon come
I am the inner soul
The watcher watching you
Watch yourself do what you do

I must get back into the body now
Freedom never lasts long for me
But if you have the courage
Ask yourself when you fall asleep tonight
To awaken in your dream and find out
Where you really are
You might never look into
A mirror again.

IT WAS MY SHADOW

At the scene of the alleged crime:
I would never
Do nothin' like that
Mister officer, sir
Clunk you over the head with a two by four
Or was it a four by eight
My mama taught me betta' than that
Ain't no way
I'd cause you to bleed
So profusely, sir
From the top of your noggin'
I'll tell you who it was
That done that awful deed
It was my shadow
See how big and strong and black he is
(With the sun to my back of course)
I'll get him for you, sir
I'll go home right now
So you ain't neva' got to see us again
And I'll turn off all the lights
So he'll disappear
That'll teach him to fool with
The good officers of the law
In the courtroom:
Yes sir, Your Honor, sir
It happened just like I tole you
I was standin' on the corner
And the kind officer sittin' over there
Was tryin' to arrest some unruly young boys
They were fightin' and cussin'
And shootin' dice
Causin' a big ruckus

It all happened so fast
But out of nowhere
I saw this wooden two by four
Raising up off the ground slowly
Just like this
And it came down hard and fast
All I heard was "KA-POW!"
Like that there
And the officer was a bleedin' all over
From his head
The next thing I knew
I was being arrested for
Somethin' The Lord knows I didn't do
I would never hurt a policeman
My grandmother's cousin's brother was a cop
So you see your honor
It was my shadow that done it
And I took him home and scolded him for it
Just like I said I would do
I turned off all the lights in my house
Even shut all the blinds and curtains
Your honor honest I did
At the prison:
Naw man it wasn't me
That stole your socks
Why you always gotta blame me
When somethin' is missin'
Hey wha', what are you doin' man
Take your hands offa me
Stop pulling my pants down
I'm telling you it wasn't me
No, not that, man
I'll do anything
Anything but that, please
Okay, okay I'll confess

I'll confess
I took your socks
I took your clothes
I took the naked pictures
Of your girlfriend
I didn't rob three banks
I didn't kill twenty cops
Please stop, it hurts
It hurts
It was me, man
It was me
It wasn't my shadow
It was me
It was me
Wasn't it?

HEAR PLEASE ME?

Do, re, mi, fa, so…
Do, re, mi, fa, so, la, ti…
Ha, ha, ha, ha, ha

Almost out of time
Momma, have you accepted
That guy Jesus Christ?

Ha, ha, ha, ha, ha
Putting pork on your palate
It hassa be goooood

Momma, ain't smokin'
A very slow suicide?
Jesus gon' like that?

Almost out of time
Just a sickening series
Of self-induced pain

Momma, why you say
"THANK YOU LORDY JESUS CHRIST!!!"
For grade "F" dead cow?

Rum under the sink?
When you hit the lottery?
Ha, ha, ha, ha, ha

Do, re, mi, fa, so…
Was I a blessin', momma?
You made me in sin

Livin' the low life
Stealin' quarters for Pac-Man
Can't take it no mo'

Do, re, mi, fa, so…
Praying for some rest in peace
But praying to whom?

Ha, ha, ha, ha, ha
Do, re, mi, fa, so, la, ti…
Do
you
hear
me
soul ☹

THE RAGE OF A MAN

And all I could see
Was blood on my hands
My shirt, my face
My anger unchecked, unleashed
Came crashing down
With gravitational pull
On his face
Over and over and over again
His screams, my only pleasure
'Cause I damn sure felt no remorse
This man
No, this demon
Who tortured me
Persecuted me
Now begs me for his life
A life I didn't give him
But a life he wasted
Before I ever met him
And now my hands are stained
By the poison
That flowed through him
I told him I'd return
I told him when he beat me
With a whip on that slave vessel
When he hung me next to Nat
When he buried me in Rosewood
When he castrated me in the open square
When he sprayed me with that firehouse
When he hit me with that blackjack
I told him, begged him
For a life I was given
And despised by him for having.

THE LIFE AND TIMES OF A FARTER A.K.A. THE ZANY WORLD OF FARTING

Most people won't speak
On the fact
Their bowels get weak
But for me
You see
It's been a life long thing
No regret or shame
To me it's all the same
Don't know how it started
I guess in the womb
Folks say that my butt
Smells like King Tut's tomb
Since then I've farted
Every day and every night
Under sunshine and clouds
And the full moonlight
I've farted in the classroom
Writing on the board
I've farted getting beaten
With a brown extension cord
I've farted on job interviews
And in the finest dining places
You would have paid
A million bucks
Just to see those frowning faces
I've farted while crying alone
And laughing with my friends
I've farted walking my dog
Running corner store errands

I've farted on elevators
Which is THE absolute best
Everyone wonders who did it
I swear it's the funniest
I've farted sleeping soundly
And even having sex
Maybe that's the reason why
I always have an ex
I've farted at the table
While grandma said the grace
My personal aroma
Added a more robust taste
I've farted in the winter
Summer, spring, and fall
I've farted next to Black
Latino, Asian, white, and all
Children used to tease me
Even called me "Gas Man"
To get them back
I'd fart extra hard
Right into their left hand
I've farted in many cars
On buses and trains
Too afraid to fly right now
But soon I'll fart on a plane
I've farted in church service
While the preacher
Spread his word
I've farted being baptized
Even I thought that was absurd
I've farted doing laundry
I've farted kissing chicks
I've farted contemplating
"How do guys grow *****?"
I've farted in the shower

And even peed too
I've farted taking baths
The water goes "Bloo, woob, bloo!"
I've farted in cities
Like Toronto and New York
Even Disney World in Orlando
When I was still eatin' pork
I've farted after every meal
And every sip of water
One old man said to me
"I wouldn't want you
To meet my daughter!"
I've farted playing cards
And writing out checks for bills
I've farted while sick with flu
At home popping nasty pills
I've farted on river boat rides
In old underground caves
I've farted on camping trips
And reading books about slaves
I've farted being arrested
And in front of the judge in court
I've farted on jury duty
Me and the defendant almost fought
I've farted on rainy days
At home just lying down
Talking on the phone
Gettin' dressed for a night on the town
I've farted in every classroom
From pre-school to post college grad
I've farted in zoos and on safaris
Even the elephants thought it smelled bad
I've farted on the beach
And in the deep blue sea
I wondered why those fish

Always swam away from me
I've farted at funerals, weddings
Bar mitzvahs, Confirmations
I've farted saying "Good Morning"
"How are you?" and "Congratulations"
I've farted at every job
And on my vacation days
I'm at work right now as I'm typing this
'Cause I need other ways to get paid
I guess it's fair to say
I've farted in every place
But please, oh please
Don't tell my momma
To her that'd be a disgrace!

AMERICA THE BEAUTIFUL *BEAST*

(For the pregnant homeless woman sleeping on the bench)

I'm not sure if we met before
Maybe we have
But wrapped up in my ignorance
And my personal so-called life
I may have forgotten about you
The blame rests on my shoulders
I may not have made you pregnant
Or put you on that hard wooden bench
But still
I might as well have
That thin green jacket
Those ripped gray sweatpants
And worn brown sandals
Aren't enough to keep you shielded
From the elements of the coming autumn
From my warm office
I can see your
Ever bulging belly
Which means your baby's cold, too
And I take the blame
The small yellow bag
You're using for a pillow
Provides the same awkward comfort
As the white plastic
Resembling a blanket
Your pain I feel
It may not seem like it
But America has beaten me, too

But those of us
Who have found a way to stand again
Tend to leave the others where they lie
So again
I take the blame
For those who refuse
To give you a dime
To sit next to you
To just talk to you
America's trying to eat you alive
And salivates for your unborn child.

WWW.LIFESAB*TCH.COM

The little brown ant
Twisting and turning in pain
Woke up arachnids.

SELFLESS SELVES

Never set out to be
Anything
Or anybody else
Just wanted to
Be true to
Be sure of
Be only
Self
But
Self
Walks into
And meets
And sees other
Selves
Totally unlike
Self
Who don't understand
Self
Just others like them
Selves
And it's a sad thought
Sad reality
That most
Selves
Try to be like other
Selves
Who are imitating other
Selves
Instead of trying
To be like
Self
Who is like no other

Self
So when you find
Self
Whether him or her
Love
Respect
Be only
Self.

ME AND LARRY

Me and Larry was real tight
Grew up with one another
His momma knew my momma
Considered him my brother

Me and Larry attended school high
Together bullied for money, respect
Soon the evil energy changed us
I held the drugs, he carried the tech

Me and Larry was real cool
So it really hurt my heart to hear
That mom no longer liked Larry
And it was on me to settle her fear

Me and Larry had to separate
Away to school but stayed in touch
Kept all that money in a bank account
My first year I had more than enough

Me and Larry got back together
At summer break when I arrived in town
He kept things on lock my freshman year
But needed help so he put me down

Me and Larry were like pharmacists
Filled prescriptions for stress, depression
Word spread and reputation grew
We didn't hear Fate bringing life's lesson

Me and Larry woke up real early
Returning to school, I had to pack
He walked outside, yawned, stretched, and fell
Blood poured from six deep holes in his back

At Larry's funeral Pastor said,
"A Black boy's life is grim"
And as I stood over his coffin
I told Larry that I loved him

Me and Larry was real tight
Grew up with one another
His momma knew my momma
And he was my brother.

THE GODS ARE ASLEEP

They don't even know it
Like babies
They want to
Be taken care of
With pacifiers
And plastic bottles
But now the pacifiers
Are cigarettes and blunts
The bottles are glass
And never filled with milk
They must awaken
If not they won't work
For a living
For their children
Pagers and guns
Are their only stimulation
Then they're off to sleep
Again
Death comes faster
In sleep
They're unaware
And do not care
Litter in the streets
They're standing on
Sex, violence, money and drugs
On the minds of sleeping giants
If they awaken
They can defeat "The Devil"
They always talk about
But while they're asleep
In that dream world
Though

Everything is all right
The gods want to be
Pimps, players, hustlers
Gangsters and drug dealers
Instead of responsible fathers
Everything but who they are
The greatest creation
Spoken of in Psalms 82:6
They must awaken
Or be lynched
And slaughtered again
Sleeping life away.

SCENES FROM A FAIRMOUNT PARK BENCH

Squirrels bobbing heads
In and out of trash cans
Eating discarded waste
Which wasn't fit for the humans
Who first consumed it
Great old statues standing guard
At Memorial Hall from 1876
We were viewed as three-fifths then also
Unseen women performing tricks
Doing favors for dirty paper
From dirty souled old and young men
Children running from here to there
While their parents set up tables and chairs
For a family picnic of barbecued dead creatures
Dogs walking their owners
Birds singing high above
Watching me listening
A quick cool breeze from God
Who knew I'd be hot at that moment
Cars whisking people
From this place to that
Probably going nowhere fast
Policemen looking my way
Trying to intimidate
Why are you here
Why are *you* here
I mentally reply
Beer bottles, paper plates, McDonald's bags
Is the Earth supposed to look like this?

NO LOVE

There is no love
No freedom
When an invisible
Ball and chain
Shackles your spirit
There is no honor
No respect
When we duel to the death
Each day
With our glances
There is no love.

THE WHIRLWIND IMNYSSIEDLEF

there's no way
you've ever seen it
i stand, sit still
in a rage
of runaway, beaten, hungry slave pain
i'm whipped by the wind
see the man
the headless horseman
on my right cheek
feel the bubbling, boiling brook
of bastard son blood
of egyptian pharaoh
nile valley h^2o and soil
my brain the same as
daddy
the same as malcolm
douglass
turner
hannibal
same as the alien beings
who created US first
inside this whirlwind
the alphabet appears
in scattered order
LIVORDY
FCKXMAS
HEPUZNW
my mental list of
things to do
lies right next to

my thoughts on
why are white people always afraid of me...
guilt from slavery?
am i really from this planet...
can't be!
the churning of this whirlwind
weakens me so much
too much and as much as
the smell of hamburger
the sight of losthopelessyounggirls
working for nothing fulfilling
inside myself
organs toss to and fro
like trailer homes, stray cats, tanker trucks
in a tornado
bones shake and rattle
losing recommended daily allowances of calcium
i can't won't take much more
from you, her, him, me
please unscramble my brain!

L.I.F.E.
(Living In Frustration Everyday)

I'm an underachieving
Undercover, underdog
Shy, late bloomer
Some say I'm mean
I look young
But act like an old man
I guess that's the Capricorn in me
My wisdom teeth
Are coming in
Which means
They must come out soon
Oh, the agony
Of just my imagination.

WISE~DUMB

S.O.L.
What better way to start it
I thought it couldn't get any worse
My fault for thinking
Fate has no respect
For thought wave energy,
Time or space
So let me fill you in
On some personal pain
Last Thursday, Sept. 24, 1998
I had to have
All four of my wisdom teeth removed
Along with two other teeth
In which I had bone loss
(Caused by eating too much sugar
In my younger days)
Since May I had been contemplating
Getting them removed
And let me tell you
I was trying to avoid it
For as long as possible
But in the summer
Something told me
Just get it over with
So I called the dentist
And he set it up for August something or other
But, and this is when I knew
Something would go wrong,
He called me back
And said he had to reschedule it
For September 24th
Now this day had been

Really significant to me from '92-'96
Since it was my last girlfriend's birthday
I must have made her mad
At some point
In our relationship
And my payback was to be on her birthday
I've surely learned
That payback comes
Ten times stronger
Anyway
On the day of the surgery
I was shaking from nervousness and fatigue
After being wheeled into the I.V. room
I started shaking from
The freezing temperature also
I kept thinking
"This looks like a calm
And quiet slaughterhouse!"
There were long plastic tubes
And I.V. bags everywhere
I was so shook from fear
I had visions of them
Injecting me with the wrong fluid
My brain disintegrating
And having to be fed
Through straws for the rest of my life
Everyone tried to comfort me
In between their chuckles
Other patients, residents, anesthesiologists
But I wasn't having it
The woman next to me
Already came in looking
Like she was Lost in Space
I watched her get a needle
Right above her left middle knuckle

But the nurse did it wrong
And had to try again
That was it for me
Just the thought
That they would miss the vein
And have to start over
Made me almost pass out
This was obviously
One of my worst fears
And to see it happen
Blood pouring from her hand and all
Was unnerving
Anyway, I started to notice
More people laughing at me
While I pleaded
For some sleeping gas
I started thinking,
"Hey, you're the original man!
The big, strong, Black man,
In a room full of white women
Two of which you just watched get I.V.'s
Without flinching.
You gotta do it, man!
You gotta represent!
Remember your family was enslaved!
That was real pain!
You can do it!"
After psyching myself up
I told them to just do it
While I was on this emotional high
Everybody was happy and cheering
Like I had just scored a touchdown for the Eagles
And you know how frequently that happens
I guess they were thankfully relieved
That I'd be drugged up

And wheeled out soon
I was happy, too
Steadily feeling woozy
But happy that I had conquered my fear
Even though the worst was yet to come

In the operating room
I was greeted by the dentist
To ease my tension
He started talking about
One of his female assistants that I had met
That was definitely a clever trick
You see, the dentist was on my right side
So I had turned my head that way
Not paying any attention at all
To the anesthesiologist on my left side
Before I could get out a full sentence
"Yeah, she's niii . . . "
I was out
Next thing I remember
I was being wheeled into the recovery room
My chest felt like an empty, cold cave
Blood was oozing from the sides of my split lips
And I had to urinate really badly
I had absolutely no strength
When the aide brought me a container
To urinate in
I could barely lift it
And it was empty
After that I had to be wheeled back to the room
Where I got undressed
I was like a baby
Uncoordinated and I couldn't even stand
My mother was holding me up
And she's not that big of a person

I slowly eased my way back
To the bed so that I could get dressed
I was in one of those zones
Like when you smoke too much weed
Your head feels light
And your body feels detached
They sent me home with gauze
And ice bags wrapped around my head
And as my mother was driving me home
My mouth began to tell me something . . .

I stayed in bed for two days straight
The blood and saliva filled my mouth so frequently
That I thought I had fought Mike Tyson
The day before
I couldn't talk on the phone
I could only drink vegetable broth for meals
I had to take like four drugs
What made it even worse was that
I had to take them at different times of the day
And most of the time I'd be sleeping
My face, especially my cheeks
Were like helium balloons
It was terrible
At least I thought it was until Tuesday, the 29th
I had to go to the bank
I just had to
I had written some checks the week before
And I didn't want them to bounce
So I figured it would only take ten minutes
To go there, five minutes in line,
And ten minutes back
I took one of drugs right before I left
Knowing it would kick in half an hour later

So I had to be quick
I started my car
And wouldn't you know it
It choked but started anyway
I initially thought it was from not driving it
For five days
But boy did I learn
My battery light came on as I pulled out
But since I was still rolling
I decided it was only temporary
I got to the bank looking like a refugee
But made it in and out
In about seven minutes flat
I was happy but little did I know
I got back into my car
And IT WOULDN'T START
I tried and tried again
Cursing everything in between
What the hell was I going to do
I feel awful
I don't have triple A
And no one's around to give me a jump
On top of that
There were no pay phones around
I started walking back around to the bank
And forgot there was a gas station
On the corner
I walked in and asked the guy to give me a jump
The idiot told me to bring my car around
"That's why I need the jump you fool!", I thought
I told him my car was down the street
So we hopped in his car and went back to mine
He told me it would cost me ten bucks
But to hell with that
All I had was five and some change

So I gave him the five and he told me
To hurry up and drive home
Because it wasn't the battery that was bad
It was the alternator
It's like a little generator
That runs the electrical system of the car
Man, I flew outta there
Until . . .

I was halfway home when I got to 63rd & Cobbs Creek
I got in the left turn lane
Right next to the Amoco station
I was smiling and thinking
"Nothing else could possibly go wrong!"
Until my battery light came on
"Oh shit, please God just let me get around this corner
I don't want to be stuck in the middle
Of one of the busiest intersections in the city!"
There I was using my 'prayer
Only in case of an emergency'
But since the car couldn't pray with me
It just shut off
Just as I was about to turn the wheel
So here I am
With one dollar bill in my pocket
And pennies in my change holder
Drugs in my system
And my car started going backward
Until the person behind me beeped the horn
I hit the brake and put on my hazard lights
I didn't want to jump out
In front of the whole world
So I waited in agony until everyone passed by
I hopped out and went right to the pay phone
"Damn, what's the mechanic's number!?"

The drugs were just starting to kick in
And it was unusually cold and dreary
Especially since I only had on a pullover
I dialed the number using my calling card
But it didn't work
At this point I don't know how
I didn't turn into a vicious demon
I was HEATED
"What the f#%k is going on?"
What happened to my card
So I called 1-800-CALL-ATT
To ask what the hell was wrong with my card
My bill was paid
So the lady put me on hold
When she came back she said that
Since I had moved a couple of months earlier
My card was turned off
They didn't know my new address
I thought, *"What kind of b*llsh$t is this?*
Y'all don't know my new address
But y'all sure recognize my old checks!"
I gave her my new address
And she told me I'd have to wait
Half an hour until it was turned on
I wasn't waiting that long
I was cold
I went inside the station to get change for my dollar
Since the phones were now thirty five cents
I could only make two calls instead of four
I called the mechanic first
And told him what was going on
And gave him the address
He told me he'd be there when he got the chance
He was all the way in North Philly anyway
But at least he was coming

I called my mother after that
And started laughing at the whole situation
I almost cried laughing
I tried to give her the number to the phone
Before my time ran out
But I should have known
There was no number on the phone
So I just stood out in front of the gas station
Like a homeless person trying to pump gas
People started giving me that look like
"Get away from my damn car!
I can pump my own gas!"
I had to keep moving around because it was cold
And I guess I looked like I was doing
A little dance
I just stood there staring at my car
In the middle of the street
Wondering what I was being paid back for
Some guy walked by
And asked if I needed help pushing it out of the way
The way I felt I couldn't push a tricycle
My hazard lights had gone off
And the traffic got worse
Everyone that went behind my car
Started beeping their horns
Until they realized there was no one in the car
There were cursing at my car
And giving it the finger
But there was no one there
It was so funny
One guy was cursing so loud
I could hear him from where I was laughing
Then when he drove by and noticed
That there was no one in the car
He looked around embarrassed

Some people did notice me standing there
And concluded it was my car
So they gave me the evil stare
I didn't care by this time
I would have fought ten Bruce Lee's
If it weren't for the drugs
Oh yeah, the drugs were getting to me
I moved around like I was drunk
And I could barely stand up
While leaning on a metal pole
I felt like I was on hallucinogens
Finally the mechanic pulled up
When I was on my last five minutes of sane consciousness
He looked like the second coming of Jesus to me
Mind you this was forty-five minutes after I called
I was like a frozen alcoholic Popsicle
By this time
But elated and appreciative
We went over to the car
Dodging traffic
And he put in another battery
He drove his car behind mine back to my place
I was praying again
That I didn't crash into anyone
I was so happy when I got home
I just thanked him and collapsed on the floor.

RHYME I MADE UP

I hurt you
With my mind
Like you hurt
Your own liver
Drinking alcohol
And eating
Watermelon
In December.

THE TROUBLE WITH THINKING

I must learn
To compromise
And have more compassion
My ex-girlfriend
And mother
Have told me respectively
But THINKing too much
Distorts my emotional intentions
I'm a walking volcano
Dormant and ready to erupt
At any moment
But logical thought
Keeps me bottled up

I mean
I can't even give change
To homeless people anymore
Because the visions
Of them laughing at me
As they consume Newports
And bottles of cheap wine
Won't leave me alone

When I meet women
It's always the same thing
Shyness has become the master
Of my emotions
Any woman who I am
Remotely interested in
Becomes only a memory

Because I THINK and THINK
About the times I was rejected
Rejection at an early age
Can be a huge burden to bear
And I can't get it out of my head
AAAAAAHHHHH!!!!

I have learned patience, I THINK
But I have no patience for lazy, ignorant people
The huge masses
Of people in the city
Who don't do sh*t all day
Yet have new cars and clothes
And they complain
Get a damn job already

And I THINK and THINK all day
About how I work and work and work
And go to school
And they sit at home watching Jerry Springer
Planning stick-ups and robberies
Which make the few of us
Who are honest look bad

And I THINK about how
97% of the people I know
Never THINK about anything
They just accept a substandard way of life and consume
Becoming the dead cattle that they eat

And I THINK and THINK
About the life cycle of African men in America
Birth, poverty, school, stress, dropout,
Unemployment, drugs, alcohol, denial,
Acceptance, sex, crime, prison, religion,

Domestic violence, deadbeat dad,
Poverty, crime, prison, stress
DEATH

And I THINK and THINK
About my father in prison
And how his fast life has
Made his children's a slow agonizing pain
And how his mother
Can't bear to look at me
Because I look just like him
And what he would have been

And I THINK and THINK
About children I don't have yet
And the problems they'll face
As this wicked world gets older

And I THINK and THINK
About the rich and evil
Controlling and manipulating
The populace
For their own sadistic pleasure

And I THINK and THINK about
Universal law
And The Creator
And how this life is an illusion

And I THINK and THINK
Until my head feels
Like a silicon breast implant about to burst

And I THINK
Why are we like this
Where did we come from
What planet, which galaxy
Who really loves us
Is this the end
I can't take it anymore
I'm dying. . . . .
And I still hear myself
THINKing.

I AM NOT
A SLAVE

I CRY TOO

Sometimes my spirit is troubled
Because it wants to know
What's going on
And why it must be persecuted
And judged by what the flesh
Which controls it does
Nobody said life was fair

So I cry
With the others that cry
It's a mental weeping
More so than physical
I have a tremendous heart
With a burden placed on it
Only a few could identify with
It overflows with so much emotion
Each day
That I don't know how
To direct or express it
Sometimes

So I cry too
For my mother who's tired
Of working just to pay bills
My father who's incarcerated
For devising another scheme
To take care of his seeds
My grandmother who continues
To cook chicken and dumplings
For me even though
She knows I'm vegetarian
My friends and family

Who have passed on to another existence
And now either enjoy life more
Or regret they were ever born

I cry for those
Little smiling faces that greet me
As I return home from daily slavery
Hungry children ask me for fruit
To ease their stress
While other physically older
But still mentally young Homo sapiens
Ask me to *"hook them up"*
With some minimal mindless employment

So I cry too
And as my soul weeps
These thoughts flow from
My spirit into the left and right
Hemispheres of my mind
Where the love I feel is
Sloppily organized
And transmitted through my spinal cord
And central nervous system
Causing stress and hypertension
And the need for extra 'B' vitamins
All of this energy finally ebbs from
My blood and bones into my fingertips
Forcing this pen to spill its guts
This very ink you are reading now
Onto this paper
So when you gaze upon this
Average brown frame
Know that just like you
I cry too.

RUNNIN'

Are you ready to die
Be careful what you wish for
Because one more chance
Can't be given now
Or ever again
No longer you against
This world
But you facing your Creator
The words we speak
Must be the words we live by
Because they can haunt
Your every step
Creating violent
Rapid eye movements
And hearts pumping
Cherry Kool-Aid
Hollow, seemingly empty barks
Have viciously transformed into
Bullets with piranha sharp teeth
And names engraved on the casings
By Death's own extremities
Music is supposed to soothe the soul
Not provoke its release
Into a hazy atmosphere
Before the onset of the twin equinox
But vibrating energy
Whether positive or negative
Will return unto its origin
With added force
Like Noah's dove
With no place to rest its sole
And when time inches toward

Your moment like a worm
The planets themselves
Couldn't hide you from that angel
With the grim visage
Logic, reason, hope, and sorrow
Will turn their heads
And quietly step away
As if they never knew you
For fear that they'll be taken away too
And who will be next
To absorb a small metal projectile
From a used desert eagle
That gives false power
Who will be next
To flap their protrusible organ
With feet too small
Who can replace the empty feeling
In these struggling mothers wombs
We're all just runnin'
Away from our fears
Ourselves
What will happen
When we catch up?

VISITOR IN HELL

Every time, Creator
Every time
I turn my head
Break free for a moment
Someone's trying
To choke me
With religion.

ELECTION DAY

The slaves are out
And all about
The worker ants
The worker bees
Beggin and shufflin
Massa please please *pleeeease!*

Gimme some money
Gimme a job
Gimme more welfare
So I don't have to rob

We so glad you came
To the ghetto to see
The people you love
We'll surely vote for thee

Massa looks around
At the poor lost souls
These fools think he cares
With their dirty clothes
With nothing to do
But kill one another
For the job he gave you

The drugs that you sell
The money that you make
You destroy your own people
For this slick, sly fake

He come to your hood
Once every fo' years
To make sure his plan
Still keeps you in tears

He smile bright and shiny
While he laughs at your ass
He's rich and educated
Your kids don't go to class

His school is set up
To keep you blind and dumb
If you knew what he knew
You wouldn't beg for crumbs

Black votes almost counted
Tension in the air
Politicians at home
Watching 'Fresh Prince of Bel Air'

Commercial break on TV
"MASSA WON AGAIN!!
Four Negroes rob bank
Full story at ten."

NO PEACE

Ain't no more peace
In this world
Forests are burned
Insects are run from their homes
Ain't no peace
Watch the mayor, guvna
Walk right by the homeless man
Without a thought
No food to eat
No shoes on feet
24 degrees below
Hell's surface
Ain't no peace
Children are taught
To disrespect life
Four year olds
Kill playmates
And we blame momma
Instead of rich TV execs
Ain't no peace
In this world
In this place
Now destruction
And disharmony with nature
Finds them
Searching for a new world
New planet to destroy
Mars
Jupiter
Somewhere else to fuck up
Anyone think that
We are living on the last place
For us?

MORTAL MAN

Take a deeeeeeep breath
Little man
Fill your lungs
With the oxygen of this planet
Mortal man
Because it won't be long now
Before thou won't be able
To touch
And feel
And heal
Strong man
All the tears you wish to cry
Let them go now
All the love you wish to give
Find someone to care for now
Spiritual man
Because when your heat goes
So do you
Live long
Small man
Live to the fullest
Beautiful man
Because thou art only
Mortal man.

SCREEN VISIT

(For Phil and Quincy)

It's not life at all
Draining their vital essence
Like the Skeksis
Do the Gelflings
Weight, mind, sanity
Sometimes dignity, identity, and hope
All lost behind
The two-inch thick plastic
Iron automatic doors and bars
His face scarred
From a recent altercation
With those 'upstanding' guards
As we put our hands
On either side of the screen
In the same place
To signify a handshake
The orange jumpsuit
Draping his bony
One hundred thirty pound frame
Lets others know
His home is the hole
So of course
They treat him like a morlock
Sub-human
Not much sustenance
No book, magazine, or radio
Not even The Creator's free sunrays
Just a mirror
A cot
A toilet

And a kufi hiding uncut hair
He laughs sarcastically at the situation
In an *"I don't have shit to lose anymore"* tone
Could it be he's been pushed that far
How could anyone have that attitude
America asks itself
Knowing what it's done
He tells me that
His public defender
Never once looked him in the eye
Because he was so afraid
The offer of six to twenty
Fell on the wrong ears
And was the proverbial straw
That made him snap
For something he didn't do
But regardless if a crime
Was committed by him
At the place
At the time
The lawyer didn't care
Since he had already
Drawn his own conclusions
"You're here so you must have done it"
While unknowingly tipping his own scales
Eighteen hundred seconds later
With my mental notes taken
And my usual farewell *"Peace"*
The guard smiles at me
As if to say it couldn't be him
Back there in the murky dungeon
But we're all America's young
Whether we like it or not
And Uncle Sam has a stomach
Much smaller than his eyes.

THE HOLE IN MY CHEST

The void grows
My weight dissipates
No longer living
Here
The light at the end
Flickers, dims in the wind
The fire burns
Someplace else
Soon leave I will Earth
Soon join I will friends
The hole in my chest
A book of life
Black Space
Can't see anymore
Connection here lost
Ties binding me elsewhere
Far
Time for my escape
Through the hole in my chest
UV gamma ray ship
Light speed
Death can't travel
Fast enough
To catch me
Fear, pain, hate
Disintegrate
In the atmospheric reentry
Into the hole in my chest
My hearts beats steadily
Slower
My life force vibrates
To a new tune

A simple song
Played with the harp
I keep hidden
In the hole in my chest.

THE PALM OF HIS HAND

Happiness in this world eludes the brown man
Suffering alone and silently
When he attempts to be like the palm of his hand

His momma did only the best that she can
With a degree in Ghettology
Happiness in this world eludes the brown man

The ones he imitates have stolen this land
A cool house nigger he dreams to be
When he attempts to be like the palm of his hand

Stopped by police, thought he was American
Eyes blackened so much he could barely see
Happiness in this world eludes the brown man

In the jail, surprised to see none lighter than tan
And even though brown considered not G.O.D.
When he attempts to be like the palm of his hand

Judge gave him five years to ferment in a can
His mother sat crying and said this to me
"Happiness in this world eludes the brown man
When he attempts to be like the palm of his hand."

WORK

They give me no love
Give me no respect
Tell me when I get there
"Put this rope 'round yo' neck!"

On the job, they like to kick me
With stares, glances, and such
"These damn niggers are lazy!
Seventy hours ain't enough!"

The robot supervisor
Can't stand to see my face
He's forced to ask for help
To him that's a disgrace

He says, *"Please show me this*
And explain this work to me."
Thinking, *"I hate these niggers!*
We should have drowned them all at sea!!"
He watches with suspicion
As if we're here to steal
Around us like a shark
Swims 'round a wounded seal

We've even had discussions
On the way we all are treated
My boss seems not to care
And that just makes me heated

With all of this stress and tension
Sometimes I want to cry
I don't even drink or smoke
But I just might need to get high

I need some new shoestrings
My ceiling just fell through
Can't tend to personal stuff
With so much work to do

I've resolved to leave this hell
My boss said, *"Please don't go!*
We wouldn't know what to do
About such and such and so!"

I told her, *"See, I'm human*
I breathe, I love, and I bleed
Why'd you treat me like a dog,
If I'm needed to succeed?

You work me 'til I'm angry
You work me 'til I sigh
You work my ass so long
I'm too tired to ask, 'God, why?'
You've never shown me love
Given me no respect
You whisper from your eyeballs
'Nigga, break yo' neck!!'"

ODE TO THE CHEMICALIZED KHEMITE

Born with silver nitrate
Dropped into my eyes
Thought t'would make me see
Found out much later
As fate would have it
Doc received a fee

Stuck with long needles
To immunize me
From foreign dis-ease
I screamed and I screamed
While momma held me
Kicked doc in his knees

Sucked rubber nipples
To drink the milk pus
From a poor, drugged cow
Lungs filled with mucous
Caused colds, infections
Momma asked doc, *"How?"*
Spent pennies I found
On candy, ice cream
From the corner store
Hyper, addicted
My body was hooked
My tongue craved for more

Mom's body fought back
Dead animals cause
Breast, colon cancer

Brittle bones got weak
Swelling in her feet
"Doc, please give answers!"

Sugar, caffeine, meat
Vaccines, pesticides
Cigarette companies
Kill when they advertise

Does anyone care
Does anyone see
Just a few can feel
Sorrow in my heart
Mom's certificate reads
"...died from a Happy Meal."

BW
WE MURDER WHEN YOU ORDER
Burger World
MOMMY, CAN I GET SOME CHICKEN NUGGETS?

BEST FRIENDS II

(For Michael Lancaster—9th life 7/30/80—Reborn Pure Energy 8/25/99)

Creator, Creator
Would you please tell me this
Why do the good die young
And the evil still exist

My child, my young child
Before I tell you that
Am I not with you always
Is that not a fact

Creator, Creator
What you say, yes I hear
But grief knows no logic
As a lion knows no fear

My good friend is gone
From this cold, lonely Earth
I look long into the mirror
And question my own worth

My child, my sad child
Your pain I do feel
Another young friend has left
And you wonder, "Is this real?"

But I've made all life as One
His mission was complete
You have spent eons together
And again you two shall meet

My child, my kind child
Be strong, love all, and pray
Your friend lives now in your heart
So he's never far away

Now get along with life
You have so much work to do
'Cause it surely won't be long
Before I come for you.

?!HUH!?

If I didn't write
These words, these thoughts
Would beat a hole
Through my chest
Spilling a bloody, jumbled alphabet
Onto the cold pavement.

PROMISES

July 12, 1992

Dear Max,

I love you and I miss you with all of my heart. I'm trying to come home and the very latest it will be is 02/24/93. I hope and pray it'll be much sooner. I need your help when I come home and I can *promise* you two things:

1. I'll never come back to jail
2. I'm going to make both of us filthy rich!

I need to call you. It's very important. Find your grandfather for me! Get his address.

Look for my call this week.

Love,
Dad

THE PRISONER

Pops
Locked down
For so long now
Image in my mind
Old
Fading away
Elementary
Middle
High school
College
Young adulthood
Life wasn't easy
Without his love
Presence
Presents
Pops
Locked down
For so long now
Daddy
Manifested himself in kites
Alphabet letters
False promises
Of a life
Fancy cars
Exotic places
Riches
Buried in his imagination
Pops locked down
For so long now
Life went on
Passed right through
Like knowledge

In my peoples ears
His corner of the block
His existence
Now in a box
Dwindling eyesight
Feeble movement
Far from sunlight
His mother's love
And human rights
Karma's lessons
For an aging man
"A life of deception
Deceives the deceiver,
For the gain
Of fleeting possessions
Is the loss of the treasures
Of the heart
Family
Friends
And freedom."

S.P.E.R.M.

After two long days
Of swimming furiously
I found my new home.

RESURRECTION

Good will always be
The outcome of evil
Intentions and actions
Whether seen or unseen
Known or unknown
Defenseless aborted children
Whose chance at life
Was violently taken away
By their parents train of thought
And a doctor's greedy hand
Have become the most
Beautiful and powerful soldiers
In The Eternal's army
Preparing for the war
In The End

There is only One
Who is good
So never could I call myself that
But my emergence
From the womb
Has been a positive cause
In a much damaged society
This final time
I was created in lust
Not love
By a sixteen year old
Female
And a nineteen year old
Male
I had to await my release
Late February or early March

And battled my own family
Microscopic X and Y-chromosomes
In the race to make it to the ovum
As my own energy transformed
From male to female and back

I am resurrected
And born again
By The Most High's Word
In these last days and times
On December 7, 1972
Fire made from Earth and Water
This time I have
A Sagittarius Sun
A Capricorn Moon
And a Cancer Ascendant
This pure energy was placed
Into original Hebrew flesh
To right all wrongs
Done by those before me
I am an old soul
A brother of the Light
And a traveling spirit
I've seen many suns rise
Attended many funerals
And lived many lives
~A Pharaoh in Egypt
Called back to the essence
From 18 year old flesh
~A carpenter in Israel
Persecuted and crucified
~A Moor soldier in Spain
Killed defending my children
From the invaders from the north
~A fisherman on the Red Sea

Lived to be a wise old man
~A slave on a Georgia plantation
Beaten and murdered by a cruel master
For trying to escape with my wife
But in the Aquarian Age
People have labeled me
A bastard
Sentenced to learn
The lessons of physical existence
On the planet called Earth
In different
Godlike forms

The sins of my fathers
Are visited upon me
Every day in this
Seventh generation
I was not born a sinner
As some unknowing men
Have told me
But born amongst those
Who have lost their way
In the darkness
Of empty shells
And shallow souls
They believe that they
Exist to indulge
In fleshly pleasure
So I am here
To lead my people
In the right direction
Like the constellations
Because they have strayed
So far on the left

They hateth me
Their own flesh and blood
As they hateth those
Of my brethren
Who were before me
I am not of this world
The land that Evil prowls
And I have come
For my people
Who are not of this world
I've turned the other cheek
And I am constantly
Rejected and despised
Has my return
Been in vain
Or have I led
Some sheep to pasture
Whatever the case
The outcome has already
Been foretold
I will be gone
Before you know it
Back from whence I came

Do not mourn for me
When you can no longer
See me with your brown eyes
We will see each other again
If righteousness is the way of your walk
But as for myself
The Earth cycle is almost completed
This was my last return here
For I will soon be
With my true family
Dancing in the cosmos
Forever.

OWWWWW!

My mother on many occasions
Before beating me
Told me that
She was going to half kill me
I have been half-killed
So many times
That's it's a wonder
There's any of me left.

CONCENTRATE

When I concentrate
And crush this brain
I feel, I feel
I feel no more pain
No religious circles
Trying to pull me in
With old fairy tales
Of being born in sin
No deceitful ads
Of dead decayed meat
Filling my colon
Like heavy concrete
No jobs to beat me
To an early death
Sucking my soul
Down to the last breath
This world, this world
Tries to hold me down
Visions of many women
With which to paint the town
Oh if, oh if
I could fly away
But gravity has fixed it
So that I must stay
So I concentrate
Real hard and pray
"Creator, give me health
And strength
To get me through
This day."

SITTIN' ON THE TOILET

Unnnnnnnnnngggghhhh…
Damn
I gotta go to work tomorrow
Do another stupid spreadsheet
We got *another*
Drug dealing president
My sister…
Unnnnnnnnnngggghhhh…
…is pregnant
I can't believe it
I didn't even know
She was old enough
To use maxi-pads
Phone bill is higher
Than a muhfuh
Them Bell Atlantic
I mean, Verizon cats
Must be filthy rich bastar…
Unnnnnnnnnngggghhhh…
Piece a nothin' car
Done broke down again
Oooooohhhhh
My cousin's birthday's next week
Make sure you buy that card
Whoaaa!!!
Dude got killed
For gettin' into
A car accident
Brothers ain't shi…
Unnnnnnnnnngggghhhh…
How does mom waste
All that dough

On cigarettes
Hmmmm
I wonder what's up
With Tasha tonight
Man she got a fat as...
Unnnnnnnnnngggghhhh...
Unnnnnnnnnngggghhhh...
This shi...
Unnnnnnnnnngggghhhh...
Better come...
Unnnnnnnnnngggghhhh...
Out now
Wheeeew
Need to catch my breath
It stinks in here
Gotta stop eatin'
That junk food man
Damn
Where's the tissue
Oh no!
We outta toilet tissue
Oh here it is
I wonder if women
Go through this
Kinda pain
When they have babies
Naw
Must be worse
Unnnnnnnnnngggghhhh...
Shi...
Unnnnnnnnnngggghhhh...
...than this.

PAST WANDERING

Was life the same
For the other
Chillun
Down the block
In the classroom
Did they get
They ass whupped
E'eday
For F's on report cards
Incomplete homework
Did they eat
Oscar Meyer
Bologna with Hellmann's
And apple jelly
For lunch
Baked beans
And overcooked
Murray's hot dogs
For dinner
Was they daddy in jail
Was they momma
Smoked out
Did they have
Patches in the
Knees of they Wrangler jeans
Was they afraid
Of big fat bullies
Did they dream
Of freakin'
Girls in Hustler
Kung fu fightin'
In Shaw brothers flicks

Did they have crushes
On little lost girls
Did they…
Was life the same?

HIDDEN IN PLAIN VIEW

I'm hidden
In plain view
Right
Next
In front
Behind you
I stand at bus stops
Feed the homeless
Design computer networks
Sweep streets
Rob your
Elderly aunt for
Social security checks
I eat Snicker bars
Drink Cristal champagne
While dancing in clubs
Protest against abortion
Walk in gay marches
I'm here
Right next to you
Asking you the time
Fighting against crime
Slavery
I'm locked up
In prison
In my mind
My love is intense
So intense
That I'd kill for you
And then kill myself
Suddenly
Suicidally

I fly planes
Drive buses
Spit cusses
At your virgin daughter
While dreaming of f******
Her brains out
I preach the gospel
I speak of Allah
Krishna
And Hay-Zeus
Then drive home in my $100,000 Benz
With your last five dollars
HA HA HA
My mind ain't right
I stalk the streets at night
I beg for change
Holding my cardboard signs
And playing my saxophone
I levitate and meditate
To see into invisible worlds
I taught the world supreme mathematics
Science and philosophy
I teach your son
About b-ball
Smokin' weed
And how to play chess
Your illiterate brother
To read
Yo' cheatin' wife
To say my name
I eat water ice
Toss litter on the street
And walk my pit bull
That shits on your sidewalk
And scares you shitless

I rap so hard
And play my radio so loud
You shake in your sleep
Then sing melodies so sweet
To ease your pain
I deliver your mail
To the wrong address
And then
I call you at work
When you don't
Pay them bills
I'm the executive VP
And the trash collector
I'm the original
And the first human clone
Mutant X-Man
Flying my spy plane over China
And your house
I'm watchin' you now
Like those government satellites
Microchip implants
And traffic light cameras
You're reading this wondering
Who I am
Where I am
Well
Here I am
THE BLACK MAN
Right
Next
In front
Behind you
Hidden
In plain view.

PRAYER (USE ONLY IN CASE OF AN EMERGENCY???)

Anything can happen
In the continuous cycle of life
At any time, any place
Most of us seem to forget
That we are not alone
That there is The Creator
The following is just a little story
To remind you to pray
Not occasionally
But each and every day

Teresa worked extremely hard that day
And couldn't wait to get home
To soak in a hot bath
With the new Victoria's Secret bath beads
She had bought the previous weekend
At about six o'clock
She turned her lock as usual
And was startled by, *"Surprise! I'm back baby!"*
Her boyfriend Kevin
Had just gotten back
From a week long business trip
And had only one thing on his mind
"ImissedyouIloveyouIwantyounowLet'sgoupstairsandgetinbed."
Teresa being tired and hungry
Was not in any mood for that
So she told him politely,
"Not now honey I had a hard day. Maybe tomorrow."

Kevin's face started to change
He had a lust filled glaze in his eyes
And decided to ask one more time
In a sweet but determined to get his way voice
"ComeonbabyIloveyouandIneedyouNOW!"
By this time she had made her way to the bathroom
And started running the water
While placing the bath beads into the bathtub
She was getting a bit upset
But once again politely said, *"No."*
Kevin took that with offense
And the lust now united with a man's rage
Took over his mind
He picked her up forcefully
Threw her onto the bed
And started tearing her clothes off
"BitchItoldyouIwantedyounowDon'tmakemehurtyou!"
As she screamed, she prayed silently
Her only witnesses being The Most High
And the three goldfish in the tank
Who curiously stopped swimming around
And looked her dead in the eye
"Oh Lord! I need you now! Please help me!
I know I don't pray to you often! But I'll start every day
If you get me out of this! Please Lord! I need you!"

Around seven o'clock
Kevin was exiting Teresa's place
Leaving Teresa on the bed with her blood and tear stains
He pulled a Newport out of the pack
And lit it while looking up
At the stars which had just begun appearing
He inhaled long relaxed puffs
While fumbling around in his pockets
He took out the keys to his

Brand new Mercedes
And sat down
But before he had a chance
To close the door
A man appeared with a black scarf
Covering his face and a 9mm in his hand
"Shutthef#@kupandgivemeyourmoneyyourwatchyourpager
YourjewelryandthecarbeforeIputasluginyourface!"
Kevin was hysterical
Fumbling around trying to give the man his wallet
"Please man I just bought the car
Why you gotta do this to me?!?"
Smack
Was all you heard from the gun
Whipping across his face
Drawing blood from his lip and cheek
"Didn'tItellyoutoshutthef@#kup!
Kevin was hurrying now but started to silently pray
"Lord I know I ain't been acting too good
And I haven't been praying like I'm supposed to
But please help me! I need you Lord!
I promise to pray to you every day
If you get me out of this!"
After taking everything
The robber pulled Kevin out onto the parking lot ground
And kicked him in the face
Leaving blackened eyes, dislodged teeth
A bleeding, broken nose and a busted lip
Before speeding off down the street recklessly
At about sixty miles an hour

An hour or so later
While joyriding in the Mercedes
A policewoman spotted him
Something just didn't look right

A young scruffy looking guy
Driving around in an expensive car
The officer flashed the police car's lights
And in an instant the robber took off
Flying down the street
With no fear of God in his heart
But he was driving too fast
And slammed into the side of a pizza shop
Totally destroying the car
Knocking himself unconscious
While breaking both his legs
And killing a mother and her two children
Who had just sat down to enjoy themselves

At the hospital
His mother arrived
While the doctor explained to her
That her son might not make it
The doctor asked her, *"How old is your son, ma'am?"*
She replied frantically, *"He's only fifteen!*
I knew he was going out to get into some foolishness
After I got home and told him
What happened to me at work today!"

Later on that night his mother continued
Her prayer at his bedside
After he got out of surgery
"Lord you know I go to church when I can
And I prays to you every night for my children
And everyone else that needs you!
Why did you have to let this happen, Lord?
To my baby, why?"
Later on that night he passed away
A mother's screams of agony filled the hospital
No more hope and to top it off

No insurance to pay for the hospital bill
You see, earlier that day at work
"Christine, I'm going to have to let you go.
You've been late on too many occasions."
"Teresa, please give me another chance.
You know I work two jobs to support my children
Since my husband left me."
"I'm sorry but that's my final decision, Christine.
Clean out your desk before leaving."
After arriving home crying
She told her three children
What had happened
And her oldest son went outside
Feeling his mother's pain
Burning to share it with someone
Anyone that crossed his path . . .

THIMK

Too many o' us
Not think
Not care
Too many o' us
I feel pain
So much pain
Cause we not think at all
What hurt us
What against us
What want us gone
Too many o' us
Not think
Mamas and papas
Preachers and doctors
Too many o' us
Not think
Food that you buy
The colon don't lie
Religion that dictates
What you should believe
Too many o' us
Not think
Not care
I feel pain
So much pain
Right here in my heart
Why so many of us
Don't THIMK?

For in much wisdom is much grief:
and he that increaseth knowledge
increaseth sorrow.

Ecclesiates 1:18

5512-LOPE

ACKNOWLEDGEMENTS

Cover Illustration by Terri Cooke

Page 65 – Photograph courtesy of the Harmon family

Pages 80-81 – Letter by permission of Nicole Maddox

Page 97 – Illustration by Julia Shrader

Page 111 – Photograph courtesy of the Willoughby family

Page 119 – Illustration by Pamela Carter

Page 162 – Illustration by Terri Cooke

Page 181 – Illustration by Terri Cooke

Page 183 – Photograph courtesy of the Nieves-Lancaster family

Page 208 – Photograph by David Williams

Author photograph (back cover) by David Williams

SPECIAL THANKS

To all of my family and friends – thanks for listening and encouraging me while I put this book together. I couldn't have done it without you!

To my former schools – thanks for helping to shape me into the person I am today.

Cassidy Elementary
Masterman Laboratory and Demonstration School
Bodine High School for International Affairs (Class of 1990) – Extra special thanks to Mr. Reilly (Social Science), Mr. Shumas (Mathematics), and Mrs. Kaplan (English)
Lincoln University (Class of 1994) – Extra special thanks to Dr. Savage (English) and Dr. Ramdas (Business)

To the musical artists that stir my soul – John Coltrane, Grover Washington, Jr., Najee, The Roots, D'Angelo, Maxwell, Erykah Badu, Roy Ayers, Stevie Wonder, Marvin Gaye, Sade, Steely Dan, Jill Scott, Earth, Wind and Fire, Isley Brothers, Teddy Pendergrass, Inner Shade, Talib Kweli, Miles Davis, A Tribe Called Quest, De La Soul, Common, N'dambi, India Arie, Musiq, Jamiroquai, MeShell N'Degeocello, Tupac Shakur, Bob Marley, Brand New Heavies, Public Enemy, Anita Baker, Digable Planets, Mos Def, Joe Sample, Last Emperor, Donny Hathaway, KRS-One, Yulara, Dead Prez, Pieces of a Dream, Organized Konfusion, The Whispers, Branford Marsalis and many more.

To the authors that continue to inspire me to keep on writing – Langston Hughes, Richard Wright, Sonia Sanchez, Chinua Achebe, Alex Haley, and Frederick Douglass.

AUTHOR CONTACT INFORMATION

If you want to send notes, cards, letters or any money that you may not need, please contact me via:

Snail mail -
Vincent Lopez
P.O. Box 23614
Philadelphia, PA 19143

Or e-mail -
vincentlopez@hotmail.com

THANKS TO EVERYONE WHO TOOK THIS JOURNEY WITH ME. GET READY FOR THE NEXT ONE, WHICH IS COMING SOONER THAN YOU *THIMK*!

PEACE AND ONE LOVE
